THE DOGFATHER

DOG WISDOM & LIFE LESSONS

Pug Edition

D1737157

By Pug Dog Gifts – Pug Books

Alex „Dogfather" Luther

"As simple as walking a dog"

"Paw written Bible"

"Great gift for a dog lover"

TO KITE

INTRO

Greetings Pug Lovers!

Welcome to „The Dogfather: Dog wisdom & Life lessons" – the paw written Bible every Pug owner should have. The Pug edition is here to provide with and also remind you of - those precious moments we spend with our four-legged friends - so many of them we take for granted and so many of them we just forget due to the hardships that life brings.

The book has more than hundred special dog wisdom sayings and cut-offs from life's moments experienced with Pugs. The intentionally designed dark theme of the book that resembles "The Godfather" movies, creates this „zen" environment and pictureless pages helps one focus better on the message itself in every page. Also, please do not rush and be sure to apply the message to your life with your Pug as you flip through.

Editor's note

I really hope, that while flipping through this Pug edition of „The Dogfather: Dog wisdom & Life lessons", you will be reminded of all the warm moments you had with your dog. Only after we loose our friend (and believe me – I know), we begin to cherish the small things and wonder how much another simple walk with our dog would mean to us.

On a happy note, please enjoy every page, let your thoughts flow and be sure to pet your Pug after this.

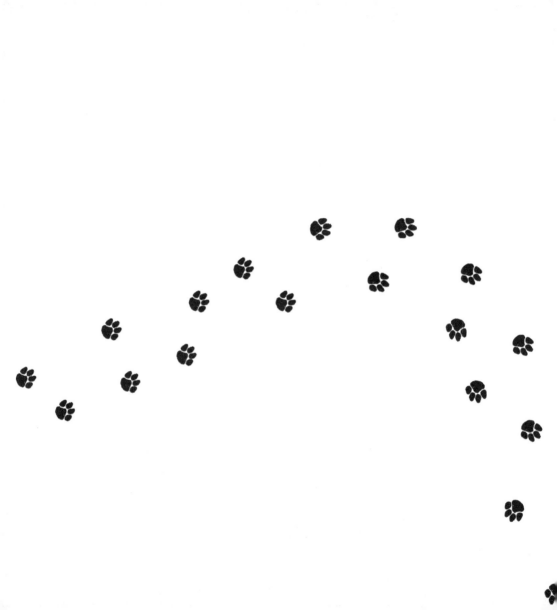

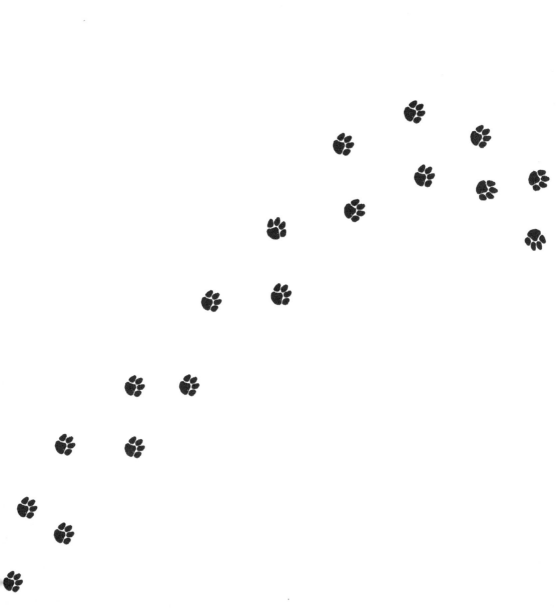

The Dogfather

"I grab her chin and look straight into her eyes. - Since the day I met you, you have done nothing but make my life better in every possible way. Do you understand?"

The Dogfather

"There is no psychiatrist in the world like a Pug licking your face."

The Dogfather

"Pugs laugh, but they laugh with their tails."

The Dogfather

"*I think Pugs are the most amazing creatures; they give unconditional love. For me, they are the role model for being alive.*"

The Dogfather

"When you feel lousy, Pug therapy is indicated."

The Dogfather

"One reason a Pug can be such a comfort when you're feeling blue is that he doesn't try to find out why."

The Dogfather

"Pugs are not our whole life,
but they make our lives
whole."

The
Dogfather

"a Pug is living proof that
God has a sense of humour."

The
Dogfather

"Pugs act exactly the way we would act if we had no shame."

The Dogfather

„*Pugs never bite me.*

Just humans."

The Dogfather

"Heaven goes by favour. If it went by merit, you would stay out and your Pug would go in."

The Dogfather

"Happiness is a warm Pug."

The Dogfather

*"Heaven's the place where all
the Pugs you've ever loved
come to greet you."*

The Dogfather

"If there are no Pugs in Heaven, then when I die I want to go where they went."

The
Dogfather

"Acquiring my Pug may be the only time I got to choose a relative."

The DogFather

"Pugs are our link to paradise. They don't know evil or jealousy or discontent. To sit with a Pug on a hillside on a glorious afternoon is to be back in Eden, where doing nothing was not boring—it was peace."

The Dogfather

"The greatest pleasure of owning a Pug is that you may make a fool of yourself with him and not only will he not scold you, but he will make a fool of himself too."

"You really have to be some kind of a creep for my Pug to reject you."

"I'm convinced that petting my Pugs is good luck."

"The friendship of a Pug is precious. It becomes even more so when one is so far removed from home... In him I find consolation and diversion...he is the one person to whom I can talk without the conversation coming back to war."

"If your Pug doesn't like someone - you probably shouldn't, either."

The Dogfather

"One of the happiest sights in the world comes when a Pug is reunited with a master he loves. You just haven't seen joy till you have seen that."

The Dogfather

"Any man who does not like Pugs and want them about does not deserve to be in the White House."

The Dogfather

*"Buy a Pug and your money
will buy love unflinching."*

The Dogfather

"The reason a Pug has so many friends is that he wags his tail instead of his tongue."

"*Even the tiniest Pug is lionhearted, ready to do anything to defend his home, master and mistress.*"

The Dogfather

"The world would be a nicer place if everyone had the ability to love as unconditionally as our Pugs."

The Dogfather

"There's just something about Pugs that make you feel good. You come home, they're thrilled to see you. They're good for the ego."

The Dogfather

"The psychological and moral comfort of a presence at once humble and understanding— this is the greatest benefit that my Pug has bestowed upon me."

The Dogfather

"a Pug can express more with his tail in minutes than his owner can express with his tongue in hours."

The Dogfather

"Love is the emotion that a woman feels always for a Pug and sometimes for a man."

"I'm not alone, said my boy.

I've got a Pug."

The Dogfather

"Whoever said you can't buy happiness forgot little Pugs."

The
Dogfather

"You can't have a pristine house with ten Pugs, and I'd rather have the ten Pugs."

The
Dogfather

"*Pugs are often happier than men simply because the simplest things are the greatest things for them!*"

"Our Pugs just need us and love, that's all."

The
Dogfather

"Sometimes I think I like Pugs more than I like humans. The only time a Pug has ever betrayed me...was by dying."

"The more I see of the depressing stature of people, the more I admire my Pugs."

The Dogfather

"Investigators have discovered that Pugs can laugh, which can't be too big of a surprise."

The
Dogfather

"Your Pug might the only thing on earth that loves you more than he loves himself."

"Pugs are how people would be if the important stuff is all that mattered to us."

The Dogfather

"Hardly any animal can look as deeply disappointed as a Pug to whom one says no."

The Dogfather

"The greatest fear our Pugs know is the fear that you will not come back when you go out the door without them."

The Dogfather

"You can usually tell that a person is good if he has a Pug who loves him."

"I love Pugs. They do nothing for political reasons."

The
Dogfather

"There is no faith which has never yet been broken, except that of your Pug - in you."

The
Dogfather

"Pugs are clearly the leaders of your planet. If aliens would see two life forms, one of them's making a poop, the other one's carrying it for him, who would you assume they assumed is in charge?"

The Dogfather

"Your Pug doesn't care if you're rich or poor, smart or dumb. Give him your heart...and he'll give you his."

The
Dogfather

"a Pug's spirit dies hard."

The Dogfather

"Pugs are my favourite people."

The Dogfather

"Our Pugs are grateful for what is, which I am finding to be the soundest kind of wisdom and very good theology."

The
Dogfather

"My Pugs have been the reason I have woken up every single day of my life with a smile on my face."

The
Dogfather

"Pugs are actually very smart, it's just that they're rather clumsy, but it's this trait that makes humans attracted to them and why I love Pugs so much."

The Dogfather

"I have found that when you are deeply troubled, there are things you get from the silent devoted companionship of your Pug that you can get from no other source."

The Dogfather

"When a happy Pug licks your tears away, then tries to sit on your lap, it's hard to feel sad."

The
Dogfather

"If I could be half the person my Pug is, I'd be twice the human I am."

"Did you know that there are over three hundred words for love in Pug?"

"When I needed a hand, I found a paw of a Pug."

The Dogfather

"a Pug will teach you unconditional love. If you can have that in your life, things won't be too bad."

"Pugs have a way of finding the people who need them, and filling an emptiness we didn't ever know we had."

"The road to my heart is paved with paw prints of a Pug."

The Dogfather

"Everyone thinks their Pug is the best. And none of them are wrong."

The
Dogfather

"Some people don't understand why my Pug means so much to me. That's ok - my Pug does."

"If you're lucky... a Pug will come into your life, steal your heart and change everything!"

"The average Pug is a nicer person than the average person."

The Dogfather

"Do you ever look at your Pug and think... How did I get so lucky?"

Visit our store for great gifts for every breed

Etsy

Dogfather.us

Available at
amazon

"A house is not a home

without a Pug"

The
Dogfather

"Stop telling me he's just a dog. My Pug has more personality, integrity, empathy and loyalty than most people I know. He's family."

The Dogfather

"My Pug does this amazing thing where he just exists and makes my whole life better because of it."

The Dogfather

"You can always find hope in the eyes of a Pug"

*"Scratch a Pug and you'll
find a permanent job."*

"Wake up. Hug a Pug.

Have a good day."

"Every Pug must have his day."

The Dogfather

"Anybody who doesn't know what soap tastes like never washed a Pug."

"If all else fails – hug your Pug."

The Dogfather

"My little Pug

– a heartbeat at my feet."

The
Dogfather

"If I had a dollar for every time my Pug made me smile... I'd be a millionaire."

The Dogfather

"My goal in life is to be as good of a person as my Pug already think I am."

The Dogfather

"If dogs could speak,

a Pug would be a blundering

outspoken fellow. "

The Dogfather

"You may have many best friends, but your Pug has only one."

The Dogfather

*" It is amazing how much love
and laughter they bring into
our lives and even how much
closer we become with each
other because of them."*

The
Dogfather

"Our Pugs have given us their absolute all. We are the center of their universe. We are the focus of their love and faith and trust. They serve us in return for scraps. It is without a doubt the best deal we have ever made."

"Such short little lives our Pugs have to spend with us, and they spend most of it waiting for us to come home each day. "

The Dogfather

"When you think about it, what are the things that we most like in another human being? Many times those qualities are seen in our Pugs every single day - we're just so used to them, that we pay no attention."

"If we attributed at least some of our Pug's qualities to a person we would say they are special."

"After years of having a Pug - you know him. Every twitch of the ears is a question or statement, every wag of the tail is an exclamation."

"Once you have had a wonderful Pug, a life without one, is a life diminished."

The Dogfather

"Perhaps one central reason for loving Pugs is that they take us away from this obsession with ourselves. "

The Dogfather

Our Pugs leave paw prints on our lives and our souls, which are as unique as human fingerprints in every way."

"You can't have too much Pug in a book."

"*That right spot behind the ear, is where Pugs keep their souls.*"

The
Dogfather

"I have a little Pug who likes to nap with me. He climbs on my body and puts his face in my neck. He is sweeter than soap. He is more wonderful than a diamond necklace, which can't even bark..."

"I hope one day to react to something with as much pure ecstasy as I see in my Pug's face every time I throw the ball."

The Dogfather

„a Pug is like a person—he needs a job and a family to be what he's meant to be."

„By their delight in being with us, the reliable sunniness of their disposition, the joy they bring to playtime, the curiosity with which they embrace each new experience, our Pugs can melt cynicism and sweeten the bitter heart."

The Dogfather

"If you live with a Pug, you'll never run out of things to write about."

"My cats inspire me daily.

They inspire me to get another

Pug!"

The
Dogfather

"I don't think twice about picking up my Pug's poop, but if another dog's poop is next to it, I think, 'Eww, dog poop!"

The Dogfather

"After dinner, he would prowl the grounds, sniffing the grass to learn what creatures of field and forest had recently visited. The yard is Pug's newspaper."

The Dogfather

"One of the very best thing about our Pugs is how they just know when you need them most, and they'll drop everything that they're doing to sit with you awhile."

The Dogfather

"Unlike us, our Pugs live every moment and die only once."

The Dogfather

"The relationship with my Pug is so much more physical than a relationship with another person. You don't get to know a dog by asking how he's feeling or what he's thinking, but by observing him and getting to know his body language."

"In our Pugs' world,

would we be their best friend?"

The Dogfather

When I think about it, all of this time my Pug just tried to love me more - asking for only a fraction of what it gave."

The
Dogfather

"Pugs are angels full of poop."

The Dogfather

"I felt bad for screaming at him... I squatted down and rubbed my Pug's ears. He leaned into the ear rub and sighed.

We started over."

"A strong man next to you in bed is a comfort, but real security is a Pug bitch on guard at the door."

The Dogfather

"I never met a Pug lover I didn't like. Makes you wonder..."

„*One thing I particularly admire in my Pugs is how they don't waste time being afraid of tomorrow.*"

The Dogfather

"Just like you. Your Pug has its day. Some even bite."

"Looking into my Pug's eyes when I get back from work, remind me of my kids' eyes and how they used to welcome me back.

– Those who teach the most about humanity, aren't always human."

The
Dogfather

"We are the same. Who loves me will love my Pug also."

"If there is a place in heaven for Pugs (and I trust there is or I won't go)..."

The
Dogfather

"At the end of a terrible day I look forward to nothing more than coming home and lying on the bed, under the covers, with a little Pug."

The
Dogfather

"The best cure for a stick up your bum is a Pug to play fetch with."

The
Dogfather

I want to learn to love people the way I love my Pug - with pride and enthusiasm and a complete amnesia for faults. In short, to love others the way my dog loves me."

The
Dogfather

"When was the last time someone was so overjoyed to see you, so brimming with love and affection that they literally ran to greet you? My Pug will do that for me – five, ten, twenty times a day."

"After I bring food home from the grocery store...My Pug looks at me as if I'm the greatest hunter ever."

"What is on your Pug's mind while you take him for a simple daily walk? I bet it's:

- What could be better than to sniff the wind and be in the company of those you love?"

The
Dogfather

"I wish my Pugs understood:

- We're going in five minutes."

The **Dogfather**

"My Pug can't think that much about what he's doing, he just does what feels right."

The Dogfather

„The face of my Pug feels like home."

The
Dogfather

"Although they have the teeth to tear, it is by swish of tail and yearning eyes that they most easily get what they want."

The
Dogfather

"What would the world be like without music or rivers or the green and tender grass? What would your world be like without Pugs?"

The
Dogfather

"Angels do not enter a house where there is a Pug."

The Dogfather

"That's the thing about being a Pug - you were born for fun. What else could there possibly be to life? Eating was a thrill. Pissing was a treat. Shitting was a joy. And licking your own balls? Bliss."

The Dogfather

"And he had a dog, a nice Pug. He couldn't be too evil or dangerous if he had such a great dog."

"My Pug winks at me sometimes and I always wink back in case it's some sort of code."

The Dogfather

"You can't replace one Pug with another anymore than you can replace one person with another, but that's not to say you shouldn't get more Pugs and people in your life."

The
Dogfather

"One of the greatest gifts we receive from Pugs is the tenderness they evoke in us. "

The Dogfather

"-LOVE IS-

How excited your Pug gets

when you get home."

The Dogfather

*"You'll never walk alone,
because I'll always be with
you.*

With love,

Your Pug."

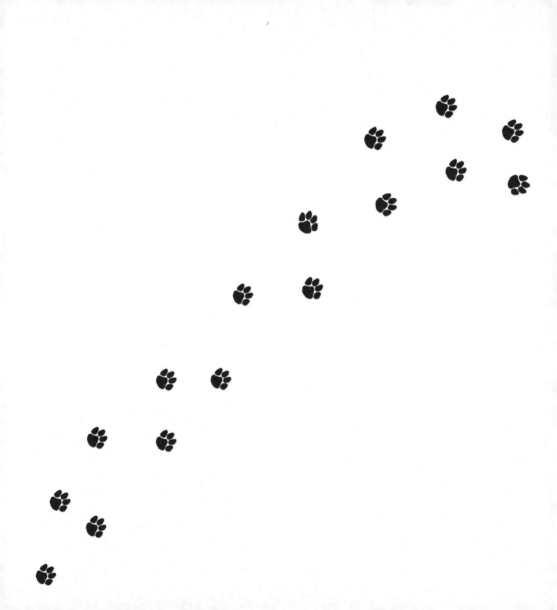

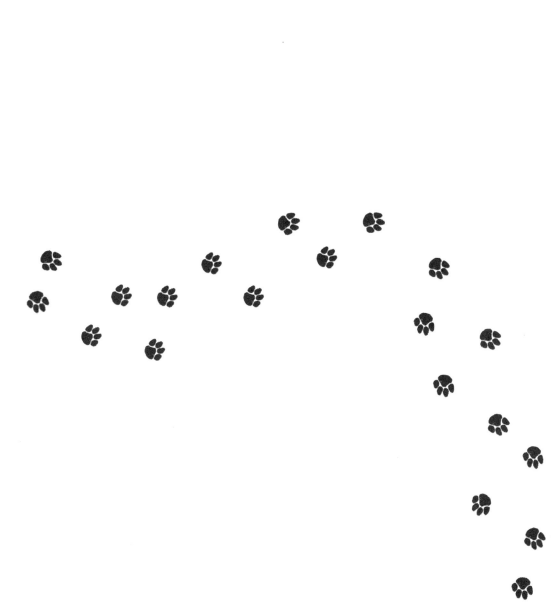

TO KITE

Final words

Thank you so much for taking a chance with the Pug edition of „The Dogfather: Dog wisdom & Life lessons". Writing and editing this coffee table book was fun and relaxing at the same time. These simple quotes reminded me of how lucky I am to have a dog – a life companion. I really hope you've been reminded of the same.

Credits:

Janet Schnellman, James Thurber, George Graham, Mark Twain, James Thurber, Henry Ward, Bonnie Schacter, Edward Hoagland, Robert Louis, Robert Wagner, Rita Rudner, Stanley Leinwall, Daniel Pinkwater, Theodorus Gaza, Judy Desmond, Anne Tyler, Saint Basil, Caroline Knapp, Immanuel Kant, Franklin Jones, Groucho Marx, Joe Weinstein, Woodrow Wilson, Agatha Christie, June Carter Cash, Ashly Lorenzana, Jonah Goldberg, Dean Koontz, Clarence Day, George Carlin, Greg Curtis, Otto von Bismarck, Jodi Picoult, Ernest Thompson Seton, Gordon Korman, Doris Day, Roger A. Caras, Robert Benchley, Stanley Coren, Agnes Turnbull, Dwight Eisenhower, Dorothy Hinshaw, Sue Murphy, Alexander Pope, Ann Landers, W.R. Koehler.

Made in the USA
Las Vegas, NV
14 April 2023

70593660R00157